PRINCESS LILY

BARBARA BAZILIAN *and* JUDITH FINE

illustrated by BARBARA BAZILIAN

WHISPERING COYOTE PRESS
Dallas

Many thanks to dreams, sisters, Stan, Rick,
and of course, Kim and Lou

Published by Whispering Coyote Press
300 Crescent Court, Suite 860, Dallas, TX 75201

Text was set in 16-point Goudy Old Style.
Book production and design by *The Kids at Our House*
10 9 8 7 6 5 4 3 2 1
Printed in Hong Kong

Library of Congress Cataloging–in–Publication Data

Bazilian, Barbara, 1933-
    Princess Lily / written by Barbara Bazilian and Judith Fine ; illustrated by
Barbara Bazilian.
        p.   cm.
    Summary: A kindly king and queen run afoul of an evil sorcerer when they fail
to invite him to celebrate the birth of their long awaited princess.
    ISBN 1-58089-010-5 (hc)
[1. Princesses—Fiction.   2. Kings, queens, rulers, etc.—Fiction.   3. Wizards—
Fiction.   4. Fairy tales.]   I. Title.
PZ8.B365Pr   1998
[Fic]—dc21   98-14727
                                                                      CIP
                                                                       AC

To Maura, our Princess Lily,
and to our mother, who has always believed in us

There once was a fortunate country ruled by a kindly queen named Estella and a gentle king named Jared. This bright and sunny kingdom was separated by high jagged mountains from a cold and mysterious land ruled by a sorcerer named Maxum.

Maxum was a bitter old man whose heart was frozen. He felt no love for anyone and his subjects had come to fear him. Through his crystal ball, the envious Maxum would watch Estella and Jared as they ruled their kingdom. It angered him to see how the people admired and loved their king and queen.

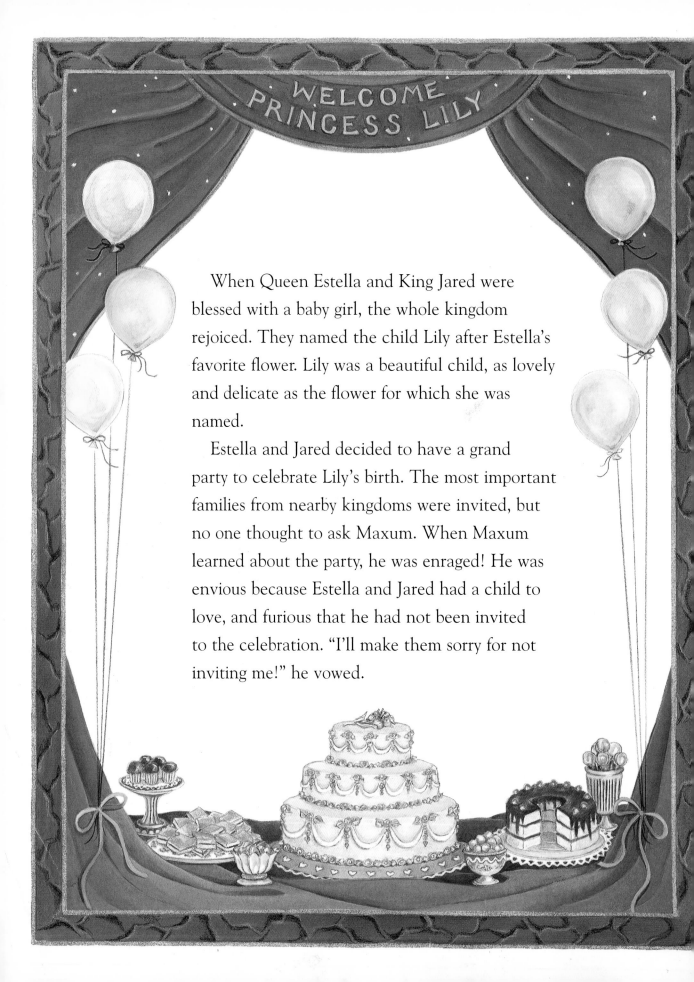

When Queen Estella and King Jared were
blessed with a baby girl, the whole kingdom
rejoiced. They named the child Lily after Estella's
favorite flower. Lily was a beautiful child, as lovely
and delicate as the flower for which she was
named.

Estella and Jared decided to have a grand
party to celebrate Lily's birth. The most important
families from nearby kingdoms were invited, but
no one thought to ask Maxum. When Maxum
learned about the party, he was enraged! He was
envious because Estella and Jared had a child to
love, and furious that he had not been invited
to the celebration. "I'll make them sorry for not
inviting me!" he vowed.

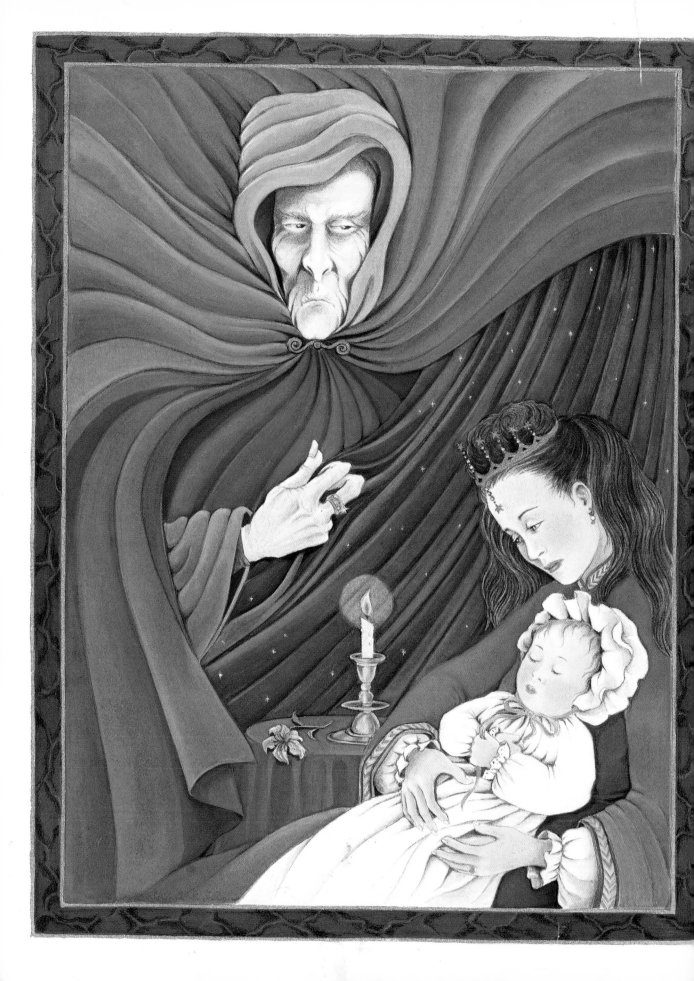

The party was a grand and festive affair. The royal musicians played and sang, and waiters served a variety of tasty dishes. When everyone had gone home, Estella and Jared sat talking quietly in Lily's nursery. Suddenly, Estella grabbed Jared's arm and pointed to a thick shadow gathering in the room. "Jared, what's that strange shadow? Look, it's getting larger!"

Out of the shadow stepped a man draped in a dark cloak and hood. In a soft but terrible voice, he said, "I am Maxum, great sorcerer and ruler. You have insulted me deeply by not inviting me to your celebration, and I am here to repay you!"

Pointing a long bony finger at Lily, Maxum threatened, "Guard her well, for someday I will return and take her through the Ring of Fire to my country of ice and cold. There she will become my daughter and never return to you!" With these words, Maxum stepped back into the dark shadow and disappeared.

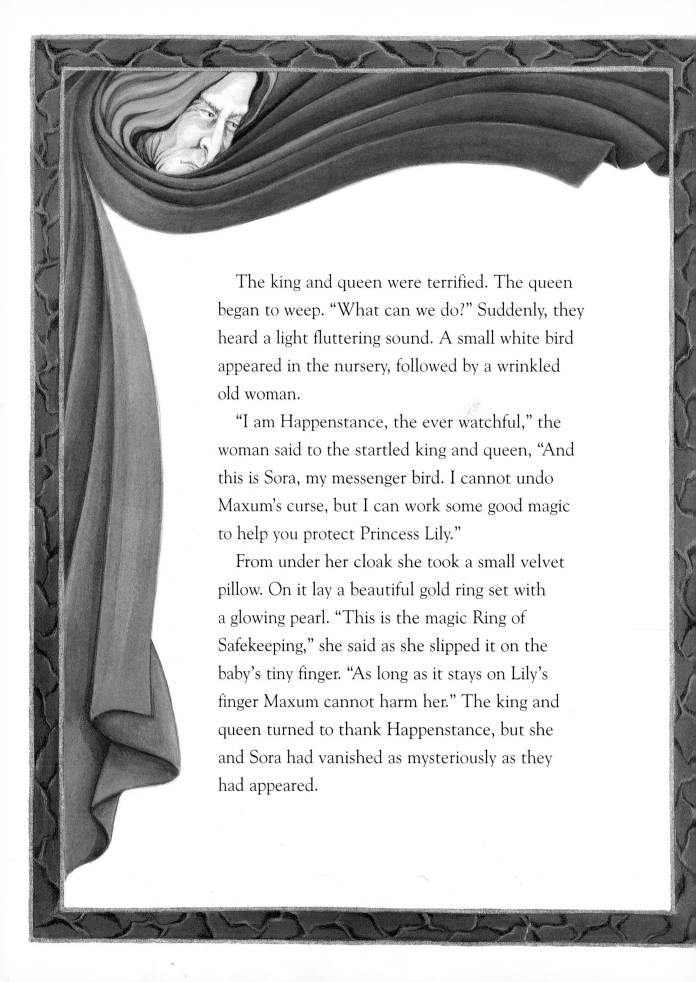

The king and queen were terrified. The queen began to weep. "What can we do?" Suddenly, they heard a light fluttering sound. A small white bird appeared in the nursery, followed by a wrinkled old woman.

"I am Happenstance, the ever watchful," the woman said to the startled king and queen, "And this is Sora, my messenger bird. I cannot undo Maxum's curse, but I can work some good magic to help you protect Princess Lily."

From under her cloak she took a small velvet pillow. On it lay a beautiful gold ring set with a glowing pearl. "This is the magic Ring of Safekeeping," she said as she slipped it on the baby's tiny finger. "As long as it stays on Lily's finger Maxum cannot harm her." The king and queen turned to thank Happenstance, but she and Sora had vanished as mysteriously as they had appeared.

And so time passed. Lily grew into a lovely girl who was cherished by those in the palace and across the kingdom. The Ring of Safekeeping was always on Lily's finger, magically changing size as she grew. The king and queen and the royal servants kept reminding her to wear the ring night and day. "It will keep you safe," they said, "You must never take it off."

"I promise," Lily always answered, and she kept her word.

Over the years, King Jared and Queen Estella stopped worrying so much about the sorcerer's threat. But unknown to them, Maxum often watched Lily through his crystal ball, waiting for an unguarded moment when she wasn't wearing the ring.

Life in the palace proceeded uneventfully, day after day, and year after year. Lily was becoming a lovely young woman, beautiful in spirit as well as face and form.

One summer day Lily was in the palace kitchen eating some cookies when the cook, Mrs. Pinnypenny, remarked, "If only I had time to go to the royal forest and pick some of the strawberries growing there, I could make a wonderful dessert for the royal family!"

Lily decided it would be fun to surprise Mrs. Pinnypenny with a basket of the delicious strawberries. She could almost taste the tarts and pies Mrs. Pinnypenny would bake! She slipped out of the kitchen, grabbed a basket from the pantry, and set out for the royal forest.

The ripe berries looked delicious and Lily happily began picking them. By the time her basket was full, her hands were stained with berry juice. "I can't go home looking like this," she thought. "I've got to wash my hands." She found a small stream, dipped her hands in the clear water, and began to rub them together.

Before she realized what was happening, the Ring of Safekeeping slipped from her finger, and fell into the stream. "My ring!" Lily cried. "I've lost my ring!" Frantically, she reached into the water and felt around for her ring, but it had fallen to the bottom, and disappeared.

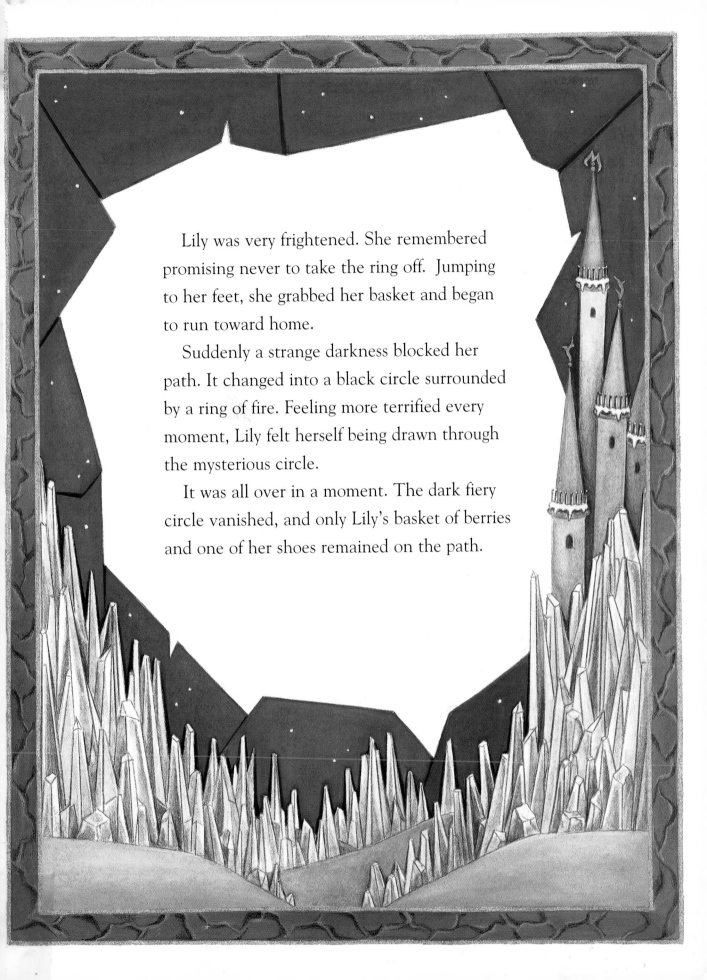

Lily was very frightened. She remembered promising never to take the ring off. Jumping to her feet, she grabbed her basket and began to run toward home.

Suddenly a strange darkness blocked her path. It changed into a black circle surrounded by a ring of fire. Feeling more terrified every moment, Lily felt herself being drawn through the mysterious circle.

It was all over in a moment. The dark fiery circle vanished, and only Lily's basket of berries and one of her shoes remained on the path.

When Lily did not appear for her lessons that afternoon, Estella and Jared summoned the servants and sent them looking for her. They searched every nook and cranny of the palace and grounds, but the princess was nowhere to be found. As night approached, the servants lit torches and headed toward the royal forest. There they discovered Lily's basket and shoe. Sadly they carried these objects back to the king and queen.

Estella and Jared grew deathly pale when they saw the basket and shoe. "I fear that Maxum has taken our daughter as he threatened so long ago," the queen wept.

And that is what had happened to Lily. After being drawn through the Circle of Fire, she found herself in Maxum's cold and gloomy castle. She wept and begged Maxum to let her go home, but he simply replied, "This is your home now."

Maxum gave Lily warm clothing, books, and games. Although she tried to make the best of her life, Lily missed her parents terribly. But even through her own sadness she could see that the old sorcerer was lonely and unhappy, and her heart went out to him. Sometimes she read to him or told him stories. Ever so slowly, a strange kind of friendship began to grow between them.

After a while, Jared and Estella began to accept the fact that Lily was really gone. And so one summer day, the queen went outside to Lily's favorite place in the palace gardens. There she wept for her daughter.

As each tear touched the ground, a beautiful lily sprang up until Estella was surrounded by the lovely flowers for which her daughter had been named. Throughout the summer, lilies bloomed in great numbers. As each flower died, it was quickly replaced by another, even more beautiful than the previous one. With the coming of winter the lilies faded and the garden lay cold and empty.

In early spring, Estella was delighted to find that the magical lilies had returned. As she stood among the blooms, weeping quietly for her daughter, Happenstance and Sora appeared. Happenstance said gently, "Sora has flown to Maxum's castle for news of Lily. Your daughter is well, but also sad, and terribly homesick. In spite of this, Lily feels sorry for the sorcerer and her kind spirit has begun to melt his heart."

Happenstance bent and picked a single lily. One of Estella's tears still clung to a petal, sparkling like a diamond. "This flower will show Maxum how deep your sorrow is," she said.

Sora took the flower in her beak and flew to Maxum's castle. There she placed the flower in his hand, with Estella's tear still sparkling on the petal. The sight of the tear made Maxum realize how much suffering he had caused, and his heart was filled with regret.

One afternoon as Estella and Jared stood among the magic lilies, they saw a speck in the sky. It was Sora, returning from her long journey. As the messenger bird flew closer, a mysterious circle of fire appeared nearby. Estella and Jared watched in amazement as they saw their daughter step through the strange circle and run toward them.

What a joyful reunion! The three of them stood in the palace garden hugging one another, laughing and crying. Sora fluttered above their heads, and as she flew off Estella called after her, "Farewell and many thanks, Sora! Carry our gratitude to Happenstance!"

But Lily was not home to stay. Although Maxum realized how much Lily and her parents needed one another, he couldn't bear to lose her completely.

Before sending her home, Maxum told Lily that when
the last lily dies in the autumn, the Circle of Fire would
reappear, and she must return to his castle for the winter.
Each spring, Sora was to bring him the first magical
bloom from Estella's garden, and the princess could then
return home until the lilies died once more.

All through the summer Maxum watched Lily
through his crystal ball. He missed her deeply, but he
was pleased to see her so happy. And even though Lily
knew it would be hard to leave her parents in the fall,
she took some comfort in the growing affection that
she and Maxum shared.

For the next three years, Lily's life was divided between her parents' home and Maxum's castle. Each spring, Sora carried the first magical bloom to Maxum, and the princess returned home through the Circle of Fire. When the lilies faded, she returned to Maxum's castle for the winter.

Maxum's heart continued to thaw. At last he came to realize that if he truly cared about Lily's happiness he must let her live her life as she wishes.

One day Maxum called Lily to his side and told her that, although he would miss her terribly, she was free to return to her home forever. Lily hugged him and said, "Dear Maxum, this is the best gift you could have given me! Though I choose to live with my parents, your life and mine will always be entwined, and I will visit you often through the Circle of Fire."

And so it was.